Remembering
New Orleans

Melissa Lee Smith

TURNER
PUBLISHING COMPANY

The early days of Mardi Gras were relatively small and geared toward a local population. The festival gained more prominence during the nineteenth century with visitors joining in celebrating the events. By the 1960s, however, holiday attendance reached record-breaking levels, as this scene on Canal Street illustrates. The sea of people spans the entire street and extends as far as the eye can see.

Remembering
New Orleans

Turner Publishing Company
www.turnerpublishing.com

Remembering New Orleans

Library of Congress Control Number: 2010924320

ISBN: 978-1-59652-663-1

Printed in the United States of America

ISBN 978-1-68336-859-5 (pbk.)

CONTENTS

New Orleans, always susceptible to fires, prides itself on the New Orleans Fire Department. Here, local photographer Leon Trice captured a training session with a man jumping from a window onto a net. In addition to his photography business, Trice, along with Pops Whitesell and Clarence McLaughlin, formed the New Orleans Camera Club, a social organization that focused on photography.

ACKNOWLEDGMENTS

This volume, *Remembering New Orleans,* is the result of the cooperation and efforts of many individuals, organizations, and corporations. It is with great thanks that we acknowledge the valuable contribution of the following for their generous support:

Library of Congress
Louisiana Division/City Archives, New Orleans Public Library
Louisiana State Museum
Special Collections, Tulane University

We would also like to thank the following individuals for valuable contributions and assistance in making this work possible:
Irene Wainwright, Archivist, New Orleans Public Library
Wilbur Meneray, Assistant Dean, Tulane Special Collections
Lee Miller, Manuscripts Librarian, Tulane University
Ken Owen, Louisiana Collection, Tulane University
Greg Lambousy, Director of Collections, Louisiana State Museum
Tom Lanham, Assistant Registrar, Louisiana State Museum
Steve Maklansky, Director of Curatorial Services, Louisiana State Museum
The D'Antonio family of New Orleans from their private collection

PREFACE

New Orleans. The Big Easy. Crescent City. Many names have been given to this unique metropolis where cultures, music, architecture, and food blend to create a dynamic atmosphere unlike that of any other place in America. Several native tribes called what is now Louisiana home. At various times, both Spain and France claimed the region and introduced black slaves from Africa and from Caribbean colonies. Many runaway slaves found haven among the native people, and American Indian culture intermingled with African traditions. After the United States obtained the city as part of the Louisiana Purchase, other European and purely American influences joined the mix. At one time, the city even had a Chinatown on its outskirts. All of these peoples contributed to the creation of the grand city near the mouth of the Mississippi.

In January 1815, General Andrew Jackson defeated a British force at Chalmette plantation, in what became known as the Battle of New Orleans. His mixed force of frontiersmen, Indians, freemen of color, and French pirates dealt a disastrous defeat to Britain's professional soldiers in what would be the last invasion ever made on American soil.

The following decades saw New Orleans grow into one of the country's premier cities. Its ideal location along the river, close to the Gulf of Mexico, ensured it would become a major shipping point, with goods coming into the country for distribution up the Mississippi and thence the Ohio River, while cotton and other goods went out to world markets. Slave labor was a significant aspect of the city, but New Orleans and all of Louisiana also had a larger population of free blacks than could be found virtually anywhere else in the South.

The city was spared destruction during the Civil War when a Union fleet moved up the river and captured it bloodlessly. While residents chafed under Federal occupation—an infamous edict by Union general Benjamin

Butler declared any woman who insulted a Federal soldier would be treated as a prostitute plying her trade—the magnificent architecture of New Orleans was spared the devastation visited on Atlanta and Richmond. Even the despised General Butler contributed to the city by beginning cleanup of garbage where disease-carrying mosquitoes bred.

Additional cultures came to New Orleans with a new influx of immigrants late in the nineteenth century. Italians were especially prominent, and many became successful business leaders. Open-air markets that once provided produce to residents and income for immigrants grew into a tourist attraction. Many of these tourists discovered a new delicacy, a deep-fried pastry with confectioner's sugar, that went by the name beignet.

A new musical sound began wafting through the streets, incubated in the city's bars and brothels. It would give its name to the 1920s: The Jazz Age.

From all of these influences, the city continued to stir its own cultural mixing pot. Mardi Gras celebrations grew into fabulous events drawing hundreds of thousands of visitors. Famed writers including William Faulkner, Lillian Hellman, and Tennessee Williams called the city home; Truman Capote was born here.

The images within this volume—most rarely seen—capture the diversity and excitement of New Orleans while paying tribute to its storied history. The aim is to inspire, provide perspective, and evoke insight that might assist officials and citizens, who together are responsible for determining the city's future. In addition, the book seeks to preserve the past with respect and reverence. With the exception of cropping where necessary and touching up imperfections that have accrued with the passage of time, no changes to these photographs have been made. The focus and clarity of some images is limited by the technology of the day and the skill of the photographer.

These historic images conclude with the 1960s. Events such as constructing the Louisiana Superdome and hosting the 1984 New Orleans World Exposition occurred after that time. So, too, did Hurricane Katrina, the worst natural disaster ever to strike the city. At this writing, rebuilding is still under way, and will be for some time. But the residents of the Big Easy are resilient; they have faced and recovered from disasters in the past. Already, Mardi Gras parades have resumed. Jazz still floats on the breeze, from clubs where tourists and locals still rub elbows. The flowers in the Garden District still return in the spring, and like those flowers, New Orleans will bloom again. To the spirit of the city and its people, this collection of historic photographs is dedicated.

Located in the heart of the French Quarter, the St. Louis Cathedral and the Presbytere are among the architectural gems of the city. The oldest cathedral in North America, the St. Louis Cathedral was dedicated as the first permanent parish church in New Orleans in 1727, after three years of construction. The Presbytere, designed in 1791 and erected as the residence for Capuchin monks, became a courthouse in 1834 and remained so until 1911 when the Louisiana State Museum system took it over.

Recovery from the Postwar Period

(1880s–1899)

During the 1880s, the St. Louis Cathedral began to show some signs of wear. Father Mignot, the cathedral's pastor, received a donation from France's Society for the Propagation of the Faith to initiate renovations. He hired the New Orleans architect A. Castaing and the church painter Erasme Hubrecht to oversee the repairs. Each renovation not only preserves the masterpieces of the cathedral's earlier days but also adds new dimensions and new artwork.

As two men meander along Exchange Alley, they come upon a tobacco shop. New Orleans during the latter half of the nineteenth century prospered from its local cigar industry. Many African American Creoles worked in this field, which led them to start their own fraternal organization, Societé des Jeunes Amis (Company of the Young Friends). Becoming well-known in African American circles, this organization eventually encouraged those outside the cigar-making field to join their ranks.

In 1884, George Mugnier entered the photography field after some time as a watchmaker. Noted for his images of New Orleans architecture and views, this photograph is a quintessential Mugnier shot: four boys on a street in the French Quarter, with a girl watching warily from a stoop in the background.

Located at 1140 Royal Street, the LaLaurie House is infamous for torture, suicide, and a deadly fire. Early on, Madame Delphine LaLaurie developed a reputation for torturing slaves. In April 1834, a deadly house fire engulfed the property. When fire fighters arrived at the scene, they found a dozen slaves in various stages of torture, chained to the wall and to operating tables. Fearing a mob-like frenzy, Madame LaLaurie and her husband fled New Orleans for their lives, never to return.

Heading out of the French Quarter, the "American" sector with regal St. Charles Street (now St. Charles Avenue) comes into view. Following Louisiana's statehood, the city expanded, and this area became a hub for business and government. Here, Mugnier's image shows a bustling St. Charles Street with streetcars and the famed St. Charles Hotel in the background. The hotel, located between Common and Gravier streets, fell victim to fires in 1851 and 1894. It was demolished in 1974.

Opened in 1905, the New Orleans Jockey Club racetrack entertained New Orleanians with one of their favorite pastimes, horse racing. The brainchild of local developer George C. Friedrichs, who envisioned a world-class racetrack and winter resort hotel, its fate fell into the hands of anti-gambling forces in Louisiana, who shut it down in 1908. Today, it is the site of Tad Gormley Stadium, the Roosevelt Mall, and some baseball diamonds.

Gallier Hall served as New Orleans' city hall for over 100 years. Architect James Gallier, Sr., oversaw its construction between 1845 and 1853. This commanding Greek Revival building boasts two rows of fluted Ionic columns made from Tuckahoe marble. Several prominent people have lain in state within it, including Confederate President Jefferson Davis, General P. G. T. Beauregard, and Ernie K-Doe, the famed R&B musician. Rex also toasts his queen and the mayor on Carnival Day here.

Audubon Park was originally the site of the plantation belonging to New Orleans' first mayor under the American regime, Jean Etienne Boré, who also first granulated sugar here in 1795. The city purchased the area in 1871 and used it as the site of the 1884 World's Industrial and Cotton Centennial Exposition. After the fair closed, Frederick Law Olmsted's nephew and adopted son, John Charles Olmsted, designed the park known today. It opened to the public shortly thereafter.

These workers are plowing the field in anticipation of planting sugar cane on the Godchaux Plantation in Raceland, Louisiana. Known as the "Sugar King of the South," Leon Godchaux also owned a sugar mill on this property and accumulated nearly 2,700 acres on this plantation alone. Godchaux was an immigrant in New Orleans who worked as a peddler, saved his money, and eventually opened Godchaux's, a New Orleans-based department store which served New Orleanians for generations.

One of the more grueling positions on a farm was that of a cotton picker. While Eli Whitney's invention of the cotton gin in 1793 made processing cotton easier and more profitable, workers still had to hand-pick the boles. Folks of all ages and conditions participated in this time-consuming and physically painful work.

For those who left the countryside for cities such as New Orleans during and after the Civil War, work could be difficult to find at times. Most newly freed African Americans in New Orleans entered the workforce as manual laborers on the docks. The hours were long, the work backbreaking. Here a few men take a break and sit on sugar barrels waiting to be loaded.

The final step in the production of cotton: loading the final product onto steamships to be sent to factories around the world, mainly Europe. New Orleans' rich history as an important port is clearly shown in this image. By 1860, Louisiana accounted for nearly one-sixth of the United States' total cotton production. In 1884, in honor of Louisiana's contribution to the cotton industry, New Orleans hosted the 1884 World's Industrial Cotton Centennial, its first world's fair.

Peddlers, who had mainly come from Italy during this time period, sold their goods in the oldest open-air market in the United States, the French Market. The Spanish colonial government erected the first market in 1771, but the hurricane in 1812 destroyed it. In 1813, the city rebuilt the building which now comprises the length of Decatur Street from Jackson Square to Barracks Street.

This impressive view of the levee shows the strength of trade at the end of the nineteenth century: workers loading and unloading goods, with a huge array of steamers lining the Mississippi River. Travel guides on New Orleans suggested that visitors should make time to visit the levee on the Mississippi, second only to the French Quarter in popularity.

In this bird's-eye view of the city from the west, located in the present Warehouse District, numerous railroad tracks point the way from the warehouses and wharves toward the center of the city. St. Louis Cathedral sits at far-left.

On December 6, 1889, Jefferson Davis, former President of the Confederacy, died at the home of his friend, Judge Charles E. Fenner. After his body lay in state at Gallier Hall, a long procession accompanied it to his first interment in the Tomb of the Army of Northern Virginia at Metairie Cemetery. In 1893, his body was reinterred at Hollywood Cemetery in Richmond, Virginia.

The SS *Momus* was a luxury steamer complete with suites, staterooms, promenade decks, library, and a wireless telegraph. Completed in 1906 by William Cramp and Son of Philadelphia, Pennsylvania, and owned by Southern Pacific Company, it ran between New York and New Orleans, offering the best in travel during this time. The Cramps named this steamer after Momus, the Greek god of laughter, mockery, and ridicule.

AT A CROSSROADS

(1900–1910)

In 1843, a local philanthropist, Abijah Fisk, bequeathed his house on Customhouse Street to the city to be used as a public library. The Fisk Collection remained the bulk of the library's holdings until 1881, when the forerunner of Tulane University unofficially assumed responsibility for the holdings. In 1895, Mayor John Fitzpatrick suggested the City Council establish a free library, thus merging the Fisk Collection with a private library and beginning the New Orleans Public Library. This branch of the New Orleans Public Library was located at Lee Circle from 1906 until 1956.

President William McKinley visited New Orleans in 1901 to commemorate Louisiana's centennial of the Louisiana Purchase. While the actual anniversary did not take place until 1903, the Louisiana Historical Society, the host for the event, decided to celebrate two years early so that the president could attend, as he was booked for 1903. Here President McKinley is seen with New Orleans mayor Paul Capdevielle on the balcony of the Cabildo, the building where the Louisiana Purchase transfer took place. Its name comes from the governing body that met there under Spanish rule, the "Illustrious Cabildo," or city council.

In 1835, President Andrew Jackson signed a bill establishing a mint in New Orleans. Jackson preferred the New Orleans site because of the Mexican gold that entered the city's port. William Strickland, a student of Benjamin Latrobe, designed the building. Completed in 1839, it was the only mint that produced coinage for the Confederacy during the Civil War. Today, the Louisiana State Museum houses its jazz museum there.

The collection district of the port of New Orleans served the shores and waters of the Gulf of Mexico, the Mississippi River, and, beyond that, the Ohio River. Construction of the customhouse shown here did not commence until 1848, and it was not functionally complete until the 1880s. During its illustrious history, Confederates created weapons there during the Civil War; under Union control, the building served as a prison for Confederate soldiers.

Created in 1871, the New Orleans Cotton Exchange was the epicenter for the cotton industry until it closed its doors in 1964. In 1884, due to the prestige of this industry in New Orleans, the city hosted the 1884 World's Fair, the World Cotton Centennial. French impressionist Edgar Degas spent much time in New Orleans and one of his most famous paintings, *The New Orleans Cotton Exchange,* shows the interior of the building with men busy at work.

At the turn of the century, the Maison Blanche building on the 900 block of Canal Street held the ranking as the tallest building in the area and was a landmark department store for generations. Isidore Newman opened the store in 1897; after buyouts, Maison Blanche ultimately closed in 1998. This view, overlooking Baronne Street, shows a city at a crossroads: streetcar tracks, horses and carriages, and the motorized car, a mix and a transition from the old world to the new.

A closer view of Canal Street during the same time period shows the bustling activity of New Orleans' widest and most prominent thoroughfare. Lines of streetcars and electrical poles extend down the entire street. At the turn of the century, the city had over 173 miles of street railway, and all of them converged onto Canal Street. Theaters proliferated, and Canal Street beckoned locals and tourists alike with its amusements and businesses.

The New Orleans and Carrollton Rail Road began service in 1835, making it the second-oldest railway in the city, with the eldest being the Pontchartrain Rail Road. The New Orleans and Carrollton Rail Road Company introduced electric-driven streetcars in the 1890s, as depicted in this image of the transfer station on Willow Street. In 1922, New Orleans Public Service bought the company and consolidated the city's streetcar lines.

This image depicts the King's Float on Mardi Gras Day, 1901. Alfred Hennen Morris served as Rex with Bessie Merrick as his queen. The 1901 Rex theme was Human Passions and Characteristics, which led to floats with the following traits and passions: Indulgence, Religion, Art, Folly, and Hope. This season also marked, for the first time since 1871, the absence of the beouf gras, an ox clad in garlands and flowers and paraded through the streets during the Rex parade.

Masking possibly dates to the Spanish colonial period; edicts from that era forbade people of color and slaves from masking and mimicking whites during the Carnival season. Accounts from the 1820s report costumed people walking on the streets, apparently on their way to masked balls, and young men organizing a procession of maskers. By the 1830s, reports of parades of maskers could be found in local newspapers. The city directories of the early twentieth century, however, frowned upon the tradition as promiscuous.

Society took a different take on children masking, as they did not consider this as threatening. Here a group of masked children pose on St. Charles Avenue. Children always looked forward (and still do!) to Mardi Gras Day, with the hopes of catching treats like sugared peanuts or one of Rex's famous doubloons.

President William Howard Taft visited New Orleans twice in 1909, the first time as president-elect in town to visit Mardi Gras and the second to address the Waterways Convention held at the Antheneum the following October. In his address, he detailed the need to develop the Ohio and Mississippi rivers as commercial waterways for exports and imports so that the United States could compete with foreign powers.

Newcomb College opened in 1886 with an endowment from Josephine Louise Newcomb in honor of
her daughter, H. Sophie Newcomb. Women from all over New Orleans and the Gulf South flocked
to this school as educational opportunities increased for women in the early years of the twentieth
century. Internationally known for its art department, Newcomb students left their mark in the
pottery world. Another critically acclaimed program during this time was the Department of Physical
Education. Its first chair, Clara Baer, published *Basketball Rules for Women and Girls.*

One of Rex's most cherished traditions concerns his arrival on the Mississippi River the day before Mardi Gras. For some years, he arrived on the SS *Robert E. Lee* with tugboats leading the way. The *Picayune Guide to New Orleans* called it a "magnificent display" with the King of Carnival and his entourage of dukes and peers, forming his escort to lead him on his way to receive the keys of the city.

The Rex krewe, noted for the intricate design of its floats, started the float-making process early in the year. Designs for both the floats and costumes were first shown as watercolors. Once approved, papier-mache artists and other artisans set to work on physical construction of the float in utmost secrecy, starting usually on July 1 in abandoned warehouses. Here Rex shows off its Canadian float for the 1907 theme Visions of the Nations.

The Egyptian float, from the Visions of the Nations theme in 1907, rambles down a street to the joy of the crowds. Rex usually began around noon with the captain ensuring that the streets were free of obstacles and ordering the floats to head out. The King's float leads the parade with the themed floats, like this one, following behind.

This is a view of Canal Street from the Chess, Checkers, and Whist Club after the Rex parade in 1910. Crowds throng the streets on the one day of the year when all commerce ceases and revelry reigns. All the buildings are decorated in anticipation of the city's most famous festival and holiday.

James DeBeneville Seguin, Charles Buck, and Charles Maurian first organized the Chess, Checkers, and Whist Club in 1880 and received the first charter in 1882. At one time, the club, with its headquarters at 108 Baronne Street, boasted a membership of 1,000 people but later restricted it to 800. This club served as a chess club, a literary society, and a social outlet for its members, composed mainly of business and social elites.

The French Opera House on Bourbon Street, a destination for locals and tourists alike, burned down in 1919. Noted New Orleans architect James Gallier, Sr., designed the building and oversaw its construction in 1860. It held 2,800 seats and was the site of many Carnival balls. Among the notable operatic singers from the turn of the century who performed there were Adelina Patti and the Madame Frezzolina.

Originally built in 1896 and destroyed by fire in 1905, the Athenaeum on St. Charles Avenue made an imposing landmark. The Young Men's Hebrew Association had occupied this building since its inception. In addition to organizational activities, the Athenaeum also held concerts, plays, lectures, art shows, and balls. Another Athenaeum replaced the original in 1907 and burned 30 years later.

The Brotherhood of Elks moved to this structure on Elks Place in 1897 after spending $14,000 to purchase and renovate the building. Up till this time, this organization had not had the best of luck with their structures; they moved numerous times and fell victim to fire once. This building boasted a billiards room, smoking room, writing room, reading room, and an indoor swimming pool and baths.

Fraternal organizations have enjoyed a long and storied career since the city's inception. From the end of Reconstruction up through the early years of the twentieth century, these groups sprouted throughout New Orleans. Here the members of New Orleans Lodge No. 30, B. P. O. Elks and their families stand for a group picture. The Elks, on a national level, received its charter in 1868 and organized in New Orleans in 1884.

In April 1873, the Fair Grounds opened to the Crescent City Jockey Club. Horseracing had been a popular pastime in New Orleans since the 1850s and at the turn of the century, it became more popular than ever with the growth of this club and the New Louisiana Jockey Club. By 1908, the state made racing illegal, but reversed that law again in 1915.

George Friedrichs and some colleagues organized the New Orleans Jockey Club during the winter season of 1904-5. Their racecourse at the back end of City Park on Metairie Ridge took up more than 100 acres, with the Grand Stand holding about 5,000 people. This image depicts the clubhouse for the New Orleans Jockey Club on Esplanade Avenue, which later became a private residence.

Originally a swamp filled with oak trees, this area was home to the Accolapissa and Biloxi tribes until the early French period. Eventually, the land became the property of Joseph Allard whose plantation was sold at sheriff's auction to John McDonogh in 1845. McDonogh, a local philanthropist, donated the land to the city upon his death, with the specific intent to convert the land to a park. It opened to the public in 1854. While the original bequest only had 100 acres mentioned, today City Park encompasses over 1,300 acres.

Ducks, geese, and egrets can be found on Bird Island at City Park, an oasis for local wildlife. Here a caregiver hands out some bread to hungry customers. Generations of New Orleanians have taken part in feeding the different varieties of fowl that make this area their home.

In 1907, construction was completed on the Peristyle, a famous spot at City Park originally used for outdoor dances. The Ionic columns, the four lions, and the steps touching upon the edge of the bayou give the site an almost regal, other-worldly atmosphere. Many people can be seen even today fishing from its bottom steps for delicacies such as bass.

West End was originally a famous resort named New Lake End. The name changed in 1880 when a hotel, restaurant, and amusements were built on stilts over Lake Pontchartrain.

The famous ice cream, pastry, and coffee shop, Mannessier's Confectionery on Royal Street established a new restaurant at West End in 1889, Mannessier's Pavilion. Here, between the two pavilions, the first movie played in New Orleans in 1896. Musicians performed in this area and all along Lake Pontchartrain during the early days of jazz. The Pavilion operated until about 1911.

Amusement centers have always made a home for themselves in this area of the city. West End featured a Ferris wheel and roller coaster; across the way were Mannessier's and Spanish Fort, with a resort hotel and amusements of their own. New Orleans boosters tried to promote this area as the "Coney Island" of the South. Eventually, both these parks would be supplanted by Pontchartrain Beach at the site of Spanish Fort in the 1920s and closed in 1983.

The second-oldest yacht club in the country, the Southern Yacht Club opened in 1849 in Pass Christian, Mississippi, and relocated to New Orleans in 1857. One of the oldest regattas in the country, the Race to the Coast, stretches from Lake Pontchartrain to the Mississippi Sound. This building, constructed in 1899 under the direction of Commodore Albert Baldwin, received major renovations in 1920, but it was in such bad condition by 1949 that it was replaced with a more modern building, which Hurricane Katrina destroyed in 2005.

The Tally Ho Club is the country's oldest hunting and fishing club. Originally built on Bayou Sauvage in 1815, shortly after Andrew Jackson defeated the British at the Battle of New Orleans, the club moved to its location across the Chef Menteur Pass in 1869. A part of the original building still stands and is now used as the club's dining room.

Members of the Tally Ho Club set up at the shooting box. This area is renowned for its teal, mallard, black duck, dos gris, poule d'eau, and other birds. Today, the club is still close to thousands of acres of virgin marshes and bayous.

Vegetable and fruit peddlers normally came from Italy, Germany, and Spain. Here children wait in front of the market and Masich's Grocery. Tangipahoa Parish to the north and Placquemines Parish to the south of New Orleans were home to many of these immigrants who chose agricultural work over selling in the market. There, they raised a variety of citrus crops such as lemons, oranges, and strawberries, in addition to other produce to be sold in the city.

The Orleans Parish School Board educated roughly 32,000 out of 75,000 educable children in New Orleans at the beginning of the new century. With 16,000 students educated in the parochial system, nearly one-third of New Orleans' children received a private education. The Webster School for girls, directed by Miss Kate Eastman on Dryades and Erato streets, served the education needs of girls in the American sector.

On March 4, 1889, Annie Turner Howard established the Howard Memorial Library, situated between Camp Street, Howard Avenue, and Lee Circle in memory of her father, Charles T. Howard. William Beer was appointed the first librarian. The library held 35,000 volumes in addition to a significant rare book and map collection, as well as John Audubon's prints. Eventually, Tulane University's Tilton Library absorbed Howard Library, becoming the Howard-Tilton Memorial Library.

This image captures people looking at the windmill prior to a Tulane football game. In 1908, the year painted on the water tower, the team went 7-1, out-scoring opponents 103–23. Louisiana State University was not on their schedule that year. In 1905, when John Tobin was the head coach of Tulane, the season had consisted only of one game—against LSU, which won 5–0. Subsequently, Tulane complained that LSU used ineligible players. Due to the discord, the two teams did not play against each other again until 1911.

These hardy young men played in Tulane's only football game of 1905. The school played its first varsity game on November 18, 1893, losing to the Southern Athletic Club. Modern standards had not been set at that time, so Tulane's coach, T. L. Bayne, also played in the 1893 game—on the opponent's side! Seven days later, his brother Hugh scored Tulane's first-ever touchdown, against LSU, a team Bayne also helped coach. From 1900 to 1907, Tulane had seven different head coaches.

One of the older plantation homes in the area, Three Oaks Plantation in St. Bernard Parish sustained a bit of damage during the 1815 Battle of New Orleans, when a shell pounded one of the solid brick columns of this beautiful Greek Revival building. In 1966, in order to build a canal, the American Sugar Company demolished the Three Oaks Plantation in a swift, unpublicized move.

First developed as residences for Americans not wanting to live in the Quarter with the French Creoles, development in the Garden District began in the 1830s and 1840s, a time period known as New Orleans' golden age. The area borders St. Charles Avenue, Magazine Street, Louisiana Avenue, and Jackson Avenue. The sumptuous mansions, with their cast-iron gates, are surrounded with large gardens, giving the area its moniker.

During the mid to late nineteenth century, the area in the Quarter closer to Esplanade Avenue became the home of the indigent and of newly arrived immigrants. Former residences, such as these buildings on Barracks and Royal streets, were split up into apartments. These two buildings did not follow the predominant style of retail spaces on the bottom and living quarters on the top, however. Somewhat ironically, it was the immigrants who preserved the architectural integrity of the French Quarter. When city leaders considered tearing down vast portions of the Quarter in the twentieth century, the residents successfully fought against the idea.

The Great War, the Jazz Age, and the Depression

(1911–1939)

The firm of Little and Middlemiss built the Whann-Bohn House in 1859 for Captain William Whann at a cost of $18,750. The Greek Revival townhouse, located between Bourbon and Royal streets, represented the finest in luxury for this time. Apart from the artistry in its carpentry and accoutrements, it featured hot and cold running water, wine rooms and storerooms, and a 5,000-gallon cistern.

Members of a krewe dump throws and doubloons to the crowds on Canal Street, probably in response to the familiar shout, "Throw me somethin' mister!" The horses pulling the floats are also costumed. Securing a prime location on Mardi Gras Day on Canal Street is still a proud feat today, something to tell your grandchildren!

Young and old alike revel in this day and their costumes. Costumes run the gamut with everything from little boys dressed up as cowboys to young men in devil costumes. Normally, women were frowned upon when they masked, but as this image showed, not many women cared. Mardi Gras day is the one day in the year that people can forget their origins and social backgrounds and transform themselves into new characters and a new reality, if only for a short time.

Germans immigrated en masse to New Orleans starting in the 1830s and settled in the Marigny and Bywater areas around St. Ferdinand Street. Saint Roch Chapel, constructed in Gothic style, evolved into the epicenter of the German community during the 1870s. When Father Thevis built the shrine, he called the spot "Campo Santo," or "Holy Acre." He now lies buried in the chapel near the altar.

Located right off the French Quarter, St. Louis no. 1 is the oldest and most famous of New Orleans' cemeteries. The city established it in 1789, and both Catholics and Protestants used the space until the Protestant Girod Street Cemetery was built in 1820. Some of the more famous citizens buried here are sugar-industry pioneer Etienne Bore, chess champion Paul Morphy, and voodoo queen Marie Laveau. Various benevolent societies, such as the Italian Mutual Benevolent Society, also have tombs located there.

In reaction to the 1868 yellow fever epidemic, Father Peter Leonard Thevis, a German priest, and his parishioners prayed to Saint Roch, the patron saint of epidemics, to keep them from harm. They also promised to build a chapel in his honor. According to the legend, the congregation did not lose one member. The construction on St. Roch Chapel was completed in 1876. For years, the faithful have left behind artificial limbs and crutches, testifying to the miracles of this dearly beloved saint.

From the earliest of colonial times, Reformist Jews settled in New Orleans but remained a relatively small population until the Louisiana Purchase. Yet, it was not until the 1820s when the first Jewish congregation, Gates of Mercy, was established. Temple Sinai, founded in 1871, served as the city's first Reform congregation and was composed mainly of German and Alsatian Jews. This Byzantine structure served until 1928 when the congregation moved to St. Charles Avenue.

This image depicts a busy day at the New Orleans Union Station on South Rampart Street (now Loyola Avenue). In its early days, the station primarily served the Illinois Central Railroad. Prominent Chicago architect Louis Sullivan designed the building with Frank Lloyd Wright as his head draftsman. It opened June 1, 1892. By the 1940s, this station served 13 passenger trains. The station was demolished in 1954 and replaced with the current New Orleans Union Passenger Terminal.

This remains a wonderful view of the increased industrialization that took hold over New Orleans in the early years of the twentieth century. This image, taken from the west bank of the Mississippi River shows the smokestacks of the Warehouse District to the left, the steamships sitting at the dock in the center, and the St. Louis Cathedral, the symbol of the city, to the right.

At the corner of Bourbon and Bienville streets stands the Old Absinthe House. Now illegal but making a comeback, absinthe, an anise-flavored spirit, is made with a form of wormwood that can produce psychotropic side effects. Built in 1798, the Absinthe House opened as a bar in 1826 until federal marshals closed it down during Prohibition. Some of the more famous brands produced in New Orleans were Green Opal, Milky Way, and Legendre.

The mayoral administration of Martin Behrman (center, facing camera) ran from 1904 until 1921, the longest-running administration in the city's history. Born in New York City in 1864, his family moved to New Orleans shortly after his birth. Behrman was orphaned at the age of 12. With little formal education, he rose through the ranks and ushered in an era of reform as mayor, with the expansion of the education system and increased modernization of the city's utilities.

Through greater access to education and the reform-minded ethos pervading national sentiment, women found themselves entering the public sphere in greater numbers, joining the workforce or progressive movements such as women's clubs. Here a group of factory inspectors, including Jean Gordon of New Orleans (third from the right) and Martha Gould (far right) pose for a snapshot with colleagues in New Orleans.

Under the administration of Mayor Martin Behrman, educational standards rose dramatically for white students in New Orleans. The Esplanade Avenue Girls High School was built in 1911 at a cost of $188,037 and served the young women of Esplanade Ridge. At a time when young women saw their mothers joining the workforce or volunteering their time in the spirit of progressive reform, they found that through increased access to education, they could eventually attend colleges such as Newcomb.

This meeting for local Lutheran clergy and schoolteachers took place around 1914 in front of the former St. John Lutheran Church on Prieur Street. Although New Orleans has mainly been a Catholic city since its inception, with the influx of German immigrants during the 1840s and 1850s the number of Protestants began to grow. St. John Church opened in 1852 and in 1924 moved to Canal Street in Mid-City New Orleans.

Early on, New Orleans had been susceptible to fires due to wooden buildings and their proximity to each other. In 1829, a group of men joined forces to start the city's first volunteer fire department, calling themselves the Firemen's Charitable Association. In 1891, the city officially established the New Orleans Fire Department. Improved building construction, such as brick and mortar structures, as well as access to improved water and sewerage systems aided local fire departments, such as this one, the Hook and Ladder No. 4.

In an era of marching bands and civic pride, the Knights Templar parade from Camp to Girod streets, in the heart of the American sector of the city. New Orleans possesses a long history of Masonic activity, dating to the colonial period and encompassing white, black, French, and other lodges. Organized in 1793, the Union Perfect Lodge became the first Masonic order in the city.

Josie Arlington, famous Storyville madam, gave a dinner party at her home on Esplanade Avenue to celebrate the engagement of John T. Brady and Anna Deubler, Arlington's niece. Some of the most prominent politicians in New Orleans, including Mayor Martin Behrman, former mayor Paul Capdevielle, and Tom Anderson attended this gathering. Arlington reigned as the most prominent madam in the city from the 1880s until her death in 1914.

Erected to honor the more than 1,300 men and women from the Ninth Ward who served the United States during the First World War, this arch was completed in 1919. It is rumored to be the oldest World War I memorial in the United States. Weiblen Marble and Granite Company, along with their architect Charles Lawhon, built this memorial at McCarty Square.

The *Item-Tribune* was a New Orleans-based newspaper during the first half of the twentieth century, with its main competition being the *Times-Picayune*. Journalists such as Howard K. Smith and Hodding Carter, as well as cartoonist John Churchill Chase, worked for this newspaper. Even renowned novelist William Faulkner wrote letters to its editor that can be found on its pages.

Jazz trumpeter Louis Armstrong was a huge fan of baseball, and in 1931 he purchased the Secret Nine, an all-black, semi-pro baseball team. Born in August 1904, Armstrong is considered the most famous of New Orleans jazz musicians. He apprenticed under King Oliver and began his career in the Waif's Home band, playing drums and coronet at first. He traveled the world and recorded extensively, becoming the voice and the sound of New Orleans.

Due to increased crime, the New Orleans Police Department was established in 1796 under the administration of Spanish Colonial Governor, the Baron de Carondelet. The Louisiana Purchase, the Civil War, and various changes in administrative structure caused the department to constantly evolve. During the 1930s, George Reyer became Chief of Police, a new post. He is shown here in the front with his officers at police headquarters in 1939.

Originally located on St. Charles Avenue, between Union and Gravier streets, First Presbyterian Church is the city's second-oldest Protestant congregation. It was established in February 1818, and the cornerstone was laid in 1819, after a donation of a lot and $10,000 from the New Orleans City Council. The first church was destroyed by fire in 1854. In 1857, the new church opened with a seating capacity of 1,311 people and with the highest steeple in the city. The church remained at this location until the 1930s, when it moved to Jefferson and Claiborne avenues.

In 1915, Sara Lavinia Hyams bequeathed $30,000 to City Park and Audubon Park for beautification. In 1921, the Hyams Fountain and wading pool opened to the public next to a picnic area. Weiblen Marble and Granite supplied the work for the fountain, which has cooled off generations of New Orleanians for more than 80 years.

Always fond of parades, New Orleanians came out in large numbers for the Jerusalem Temple parade in June 1923. In 1916, the Ancient Order of the Nobles of the Mystic Shrine broke ground for the Temple on St. Charles Avenue. Architects Sam Stone, Jr., and Emile Weil designed the Temple, which was built in 1919. This order possessed one of the largest memberships of any Shrine temple in the United States.

The Mississippi River Flood of 1927 wreaked havoc throughout Louisiana and Mississippi; many considered it the nation's worst natural disaster. Although New Orleans was largely spared from the flooding, many refugees flocked to the city for aid. Here Red Cross nurse Porter helps Mrs. D. P. Achen of Braithwaite, Louisiana, and her two children. Because of this disaster, the United States established the Flood Control Act of 1928, which initiated a period of infrastructure improvements, including the construction of levees, flood walls, spillways, and canals.

Bordering the French Market, Decatur Street always bustled with activity, as it was (and still is) a main thoroughfare for businesses in the Crescent City. In 1935, when this image was taken, photographer Walker Evans spent a bit of time in New Orleans, capturing the mood of the city and the outlying areas. He felt that he had not captured the Vieux Carre in its essence. Yet, with the images that he did produce, he left a legacy for generations on how the city looked during the Great Depression.

Considered the most powerful of Louisiana governors, Huey Pierce Long started his political career in Winfield, a rural area in north-central Louisiana. He implemented, during his service as governor and senator, unprecedented modernization in Louisiana, with upgrades to its infrastructure and free textbooks in public schools through his Share Our Wealth program. He was assassinated at the age of 42 in 1935.

Walker Evans, known mainly for his photography of Depression-era, rural Alabama, also gives insight into New Orleans during this period. Evans arrived in New Orleans during the spring of 1935, under a contract for the Farm Security Administration, and his time here mingling with bohemian New Orleans changed his life forever. He later became the first photographer to receive a solo show at the Museum of Modern Art.

Photographer Walker Evans shows the proliferation of advertising taking hold of New Orleans during the Depression. Here Dixie Baking Company advertises on its truck, and Luzianne Coffee hawks its wares on a building, near a Coca-Cola sign. William B. Reily, a grocer based in Monroe, Louisiana, started Luzianne Coffee in 1902 and saw an opportunity to open a coffee-roasting and grinding business in New Orleans. Today it is known primarily for its tea; Reily started that part of his business in 1932.

Palm trees are not native to New Orleans; the Jesuits first introduced them 200 years ago. Since then, palm trees have been a part of the city's landscape, from Canal Street up through City Park and over to Gentilly. Here young girls skate through City Park, enjoying a beautiful afternoon. At one time, City Park had a skating rink, but it has been gone for generations.

Many of the city's urban poor lived in squalid conditions during the 1930s. The poor had little choice but to live in dangerous, overcrowded, ramshackle buildings with few, if any amenities. Here Walker Evans captured some of the conditions to which the poor were subjected, next to an advertisement for Heinz Ketchup.

A popular "haunted house," the Gardette-Le Petre House, also known as the House of the Turk, stands on Dauphine at Orleans streets. Legend has it that a Turkish sultan arrived in New Orleans during the mid nineteenth century and rented the house. The sultan brought his entourage with him, including his harem, armed guards, and treasure he had stolen from his brother. One day, a passerby noticed the gate unlocked and found carnage everywhere. Body parts were strewn around the house and blood oozed through the wooden floors. The only body that could be identified was that of the young sultan, who had been buried alive.

At a rally with veterans carrying signs stating that they were starving, Huey Long addresses a parade protesting President Herbert Hoover's veto of a bill expanding veterans' benefits. Long advocated benefits and health care for veterans who were hurting during the Great Depression. Many of the social reforms that Long championed eventually became domestic policy in the United States, including Social Security, veterans benefits, financial aid for college, the Works Progress Administration, food stamps, Medicare and Medicaid, housing assistance, the graduated income tax, and inheritance tax.

Listed on the National Register of Historical Landmarks, the SS *President* was built in 1924 and was originally named the *Cincinnati*. It ran from Cincinnati to Louisville, Kentucky. In 1934, the Streckfus Company purchased it, converted it into an excursion boat, and added a ballroom and a bandstand. By the end of World War II, New Orleans became the permanent home for the steamboat. In 1990, it was renovated into a casino and moved to Davenport, Iowa.

The Louisville and Nashville Railroad Company arrived in New Orleans during the 1880s, when it purchased the Pontchartrain Railroad Company. The L&N Station was located on the foot of Canal Street, across from the Algiers Ferry Landing. During the 1950s, the city merged all its railways and made them use the Union Passenger Terminal, thus making stations such as this one obsolete. The city demolished the L&N Station around 1954.

Julius Koch designed this structure located on St. Charles Avenue between Girod and Julia streets. Converted into the Washington Artillery Hall in 1880, the building held notable functions such as Rex balls, dances that featured jazz, and annual conventions of benevolent societies and professional societies. It also housed the Louisiana-based exhibits from the 1904 St. Louis World's Fair.

Located at 300 North Rampart Street, the Dog-House featured jazz performances and a floor show. It stayed open until 4:00 A.M. nightly. The owner referred to it as a high-class place for middle-class folks, where they could find freedom for the "body and soul."

World War II and Postwar Changes

(1940–1960s)

The African American Zulu Social
Aid and Pleasure Club marched
for the first time in 1909 and
the organization received its first
charter in 1916. Here the Zulu
king arrives on New Basin Canal,
a part of its original route. The
king originally wore a lard can for
a crown and a banana stalk for a
scepter, and the krewe members
sported black face mimicking
white society. In the 1940s, Zulu
became more prominent in the
annual celebration.

Marion Wolcott, a Farm Security Administration photographer, shot Tom's Bar covered with advertisements for Regal Beer, a locally produced brew during this time. The American Brewing Company of New Orleans owned the Regal brewery, and the beer was considered a mainstay product during the first half of the twentieth century. Their brewery was located on Bourbon Street, the site of today's Royal Sonesta Hotel.

Marion Post Wolcott, known for her images of the Islenos community in Louisiana, preferred to illustrate the harsh realism of life. Yet at times her images showed much humor, like this Oldsmobile advertisement sandwiched between an ad for masses at St. Patrick's Church and an ad listing times for St. Jude novenas.

If a building can be associated with the beginnings of jazz, this could very well be the one. Some of jazz's pioneers, Kid Ory, King Oliver, Freddie Keppard, and Sidney Bechet, to name a few, all performed at Pete Lala's Café in Storyville on Iberville at Marais streets. During its existence, Storyville employed 50 musicians who worked at the various bars, brothels, and mansions.

During the war, buses and streetcars displayed signs for shoppers to go home early so that defense workers could have seats on public transportation. Here Higgins workers flash "V for Victory" signs as they finish their day at the shipyard at 4:00 P.M. Although Higgins Industry employed a sizable workforce at its height during the war, the company lost the majority of its business and closed in the 1960s.

At the turn of the century, jazz legend Toney Jackson performed at Frank Early's My Place Saloon and wrote the hit "Pretty Baby" there. Another jazz prodigy who performed there was Professor Manuel Manetta, who was known for his ability to play both trumpet and trombone simultaneously. To the left of the building stand cribs that lower-class prostitutes used to ply their trade.

One of the most prominent strips in the former Storyville, Basin Street housed many of the high-class brothels, including Willie Piazza's establishment, Hilma Burt's place, and Mahogany Hall. It was at Hilma Burt's brothel where Jelly Roll Morton received his first musical start in Storyville. After Storyville's closure, Basin Street was renamed North Saratoga Street, and later the Iberville Housing Development replaced the majority of the street.

Like so many old institutions in New Orleans, Charity Hospital had been located in a number of areas throughout the city. In 1832, it moved to its last location on Tulane Avenue. One hundred years later, Charity prided itself on its history and its technological advances. By the late 1930s, the hospital held a capacity of 1,800 patients, employed 160 nurses, and contracted the services of 17 resident interns, as well as a large staff of physicians and surgeons. Its budget exceeded $1.5 million.

Tennessee Williams made this streetcar famous in his play *Streetcar Named Desire.* The New Orleans Railway and Light Company started the Desire line in 1920. It ceased operation in 1948 when the city replaced the streetcar with a bus. Here Henry Lacour, who spent his career as a streetcar conductor, takes the No. 832 out for its final run.

In 1943, Higgins Industries, based in New Orleans, built USS *PT-564*, an experimental 70-foot torpedo boat otherwise known as the *Hellcat*. It was based in Miami, Florida, and served along the East Coast of the U.S. It was taken out of service in 1946 and sold in 1948. Andrew Higgins, owner of Higgins Industries, received much acclaim from General (later President) Dwight D. Eisenhower.

John Vachon (1914–1975) started off in photography with the Farm Security Administration and documented rural life during the Depression as well as World War II. Eventually, he worked for the United Nations and *Look* magazine. Here he records a ship being loaded with goods at the Poydras Street dock.

This is a back view of St. Anthony's Garden located behind the St. Louis Cathedral. In 1831, the city purchased strips of land behind the church and closed off that part of the street. In 1848, the trustees of the church received these strips of land, enclosed the area with a cast-iron gate, and have used it as a garden ever since. New Orleans is the only city in the country where the most prominent landmark is a church.

This image marks the return of Carnival on St. Charles Avenue in New Orleans following World War II. Only three times in New Orleans history have city leaders canceled the event: the Civil War, World War I, and World War II. Rex's theme that year was Myths of Starry Hosts.

The New Orleans Creoles belonged to the Southern Negro Leagues, a minor league, during the 1940s. Here a baseball player conducts a workshop at Pelican Stadium in 1947. The New Orleans Creoles shared the stadium with the Pelicans, another minor league team. Pelican Stadium, also known as Heinemann Park located in Mid-City, hosted the New Orleans Pelicans from 1911 until 1957.

This group of politicians, known as the "Long Leaders" due to their support of Governor Earl Long, boards a Louisville and Nashville train for the Kentucky Derby in 1950. George Reyer, Superintendent of the New Orleans Police Department (right-hand door, bottom step) waves to the photographer, as does another New Orleanian, Guy D'Antonio (second to the right, standing in the foreground) who served in the Louisiana Senate during this time.

The Orpheum Theatre opened its doors in 1918, featured vaudeville acts during the early 1920s, and then became a movie house. In the 1970s, the building was scheduled for demolition. Instead of destroying this Beaux Arts–styled building that seated 1,800, heavy renovations went into it, and it reopened in 1989 as the home of the Louisiana Philharmonic Orchestra, the only full-time, professional orchestra in the Gulf South. The building received heavy damage during Hurricane Katrina and is still awaiting renovations.

The beauty and elegance of homes in the Garden District is reflected in this 1951 image of the D. W. Pipes residence at 1238 Phillip Street.

Frances Benjamin Johnston and Joseph Woodson "Pops" Whitesell were fixtures of bohemian New Orleans from the 1920s until their deaths in the 1950s. Both famed photographers, Johnston started her career in Washington, D.C., and became the first female photographer of the White House. Whitesell came to New Orleans during World War I and by the 1940s was one of the ten most prominent salon photographers in the world.

The Volunteer Civil Defense Workers prepared and served this "disaster meal" to CD members at Delgado Trades School as a part of a tour of the New Orleans Civil Defense operations. Delgado Community College is the state's oldest and largest community college. It opened its doors in 1921 with the purpose of educating boys and young men to the vocational trades. Today, the school, open to both sexes, is nationally known for its nursing program.

During the Cold War, Americans throughout the country sought ways to protect themselves. Here Colonel J. T. Knight, Jr., Chief of Attack Warning Section of New Orleans Civil Defense, and Paul Ristroph, Director of New Orleans Civil Defense, test an air raid siren. This type of mechanical siren was produced from the 1950s until the 1980s.

Alexander Allison took this shot from his office in New Orleans' new city hall built in 1957. He spent the majority of his career as a civil engineer for the Sewerage and Water Board of New Orleans. The current city hall opened in spring of 1957 under the administration of Mayor deLesseps Morrison and was the signature building among a group of modernistic buildings that lined Loyola Avenue, which included the Union Passenger Terminal, the Louisiana Supreme Court, and the New Orleans Public Library.

Business leader James Holtry, Pontchartrain Park golf pro Joe Bartholomew, Mayor deLesseps Morrison, and Herbert Jahncke, President of the Parkways and Parks Commission, commemorate the dedication of the Lake Pontchartrain Golf Course house at Pontchartrain Park. This golf course was the only one of its kind available to black New Orleans during Segregation. Joe Bartholomew designed and built this golf course, in addition to City Park no. 1 and City Park no. 2.

In 1860, Domenican nuns arrived from Ireland to teach girls in a heavily Irish area of New Orleans. In time, they accepted male students as well, and the Archdiocese of New Orleans opened St. John Baptist Parochial School on the corner of Dryades and Calliope streets. This image was taken shortly before the school was demolished to make way for the Pontchartrain Expressway.

Bandleader Lawrence Welk wowed fans at the Municipal Auditorium in 1958. Local clarinetist Pete Fountain performed with Welk's band from 1957 until 1959. Here he is seen in the center of the trio behind Welk. In addition to his long, storied musical career, Pete Fountain is also known for his Half Fast Walking Club that parades in the French Quarter on Mardi Gras Day.

Up to the 1950s, Claiborne Avenue had gained prominence as the African American commercial center in New Orleans. When city leaders received federal aid to build the Pontchartrain Expressway, the interstate that runs right on the edge of the French Quarter, they decided to demolish this area to make room for the highway. Today, murals on the pillars under the expressway depict and remember the once-vibrant neighborhood.

Daniel Burnham, the architect for Washington D.C.'s Union Station, designed the Southern Railroad Terminal in 1908. Located on Canal Street, this station served the Southern Railway, the New Orleans and Northeastern Railroad Company, and the New Orleans Terminal Company. Like other passenger terminals in the city, this station also fell victim to the city's consolidation in the 1950s. The Beaux Arts–styled building was demolished in 1954.

Tulane University's campus reflects the great variety of New Orleans' flora and fauna, with its palm trees and oak trees among its parklike setting. Established in 1834 as the publicly funded Medical College of Louisiana, Tulane is the city's oldest university. Known for its law and medical schools, the university has trained generations of New Orleans residents as well as those from out of state. It is the only university in the country that went from being a public university to a private one.

At one time, the Senator Hotel housed 125 rooms and boasted air conditioning. Lee Harvey Oswald, the accused assassin of President John F. Kennedy, and his mother lived at this hotel for some time. By the time this fire destroyed the hotel on Dauphine Street, it had been abandoned for a number of years. Three fire fighters received injuries while battling this blaze.

Hurricane Betsy slammed into Louisiana in September 1965 and was considered the country's worst natural disaster up to that time, costing over $1 billion. Here National Guard troops set up a staging point to aid New Orleanians in distress. Because of Betsy's destruction, the U.S. Army Corps of Engineers established its Hurricane Protection Program, which included building better levees to withstand a strong Category 3 storm.

A part of the New Orleans Fire Department's community outreach program concerned teaching children about fire prevention and reaction. Here members of the fire department allow boys to spend time on one of its trucks, testing the lights and sirens.

Oysters are one of Louisiana's most notable products and currently constitute an industry that supports over 10,000 jobs. More than one-third of the nation's oysters come from Louisiana. Here Martina and Martina, who served the New Orleans area for more than 100 years, deliver oysters in the French Quarter.

Mardi Gras Indians—actually African Americans in regalia—date back to the nineteenth century and represent the bonds forged between blacks and American Indians when runaway slaves found haven among native tribes. The structure of the Mardi Gras Indians is based on various tribes based along ward lines in the city. The hierarchy of these tribes includes the Big Chief and the Spy Boy, among others. All their costumes are hand-sewn and can take nearly a year to create.

Notes on the Photographs

These notes, listed by page number, attempt to include all aspects known of the photographs. Each of the photographs is identified by the page number, a title or description, photographer and collection, archive, and call or box number when applicable. Although every attempt was made to collect all data, in some cases complete data may have been unavailable due to the age and condition of some of the photographs and records.

CPSIA information can be obtained
at www.ICGtesting.com
Printed in the USA
BVHW021043170921
616959BV00021B/603